GREAT SONGS
FOR FINGERSTYLE GUITAR

ISBN 978-0-7935-9795-6

HAL•LEONARD®
CORPORATION

7777 W. BLUEMOUND RD. P.O. BOX 13819 MILWAUKEE, WI 53213

Visit Hal Leonard Online at
www.halleonard.com

GREAT SONGS
FOR FINGERSTYLE GUITAR

All the Things You Are

from VERY WARM FOR MAY

Lyrics by Oscar Hammerstein II
Music by Jerome Kern

an - gel glow that lights a star. _____

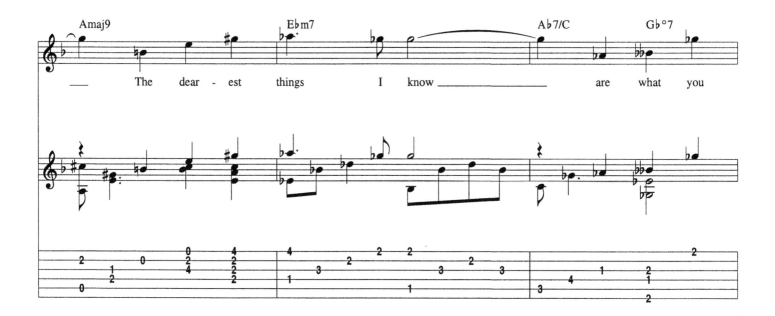

_____ The dear - est things I know _____ are what you

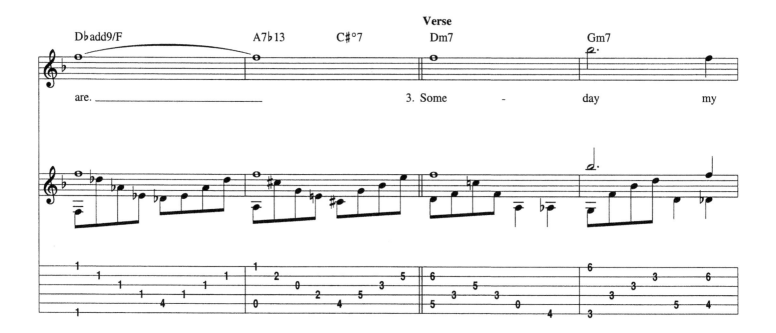

are. _____ 3. Some - day my

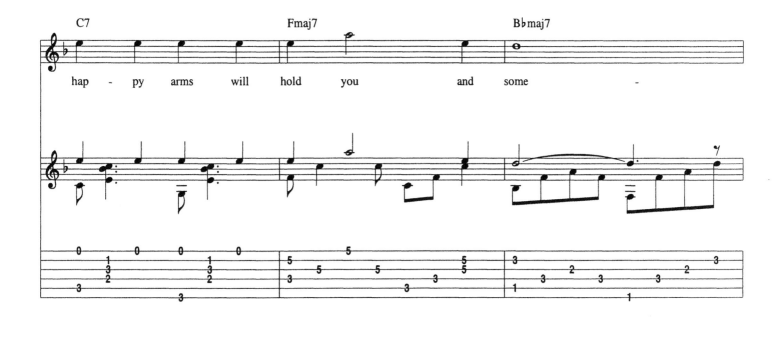

hap - py arms will hold you and some

day I'll know that mo - ment di - vine when

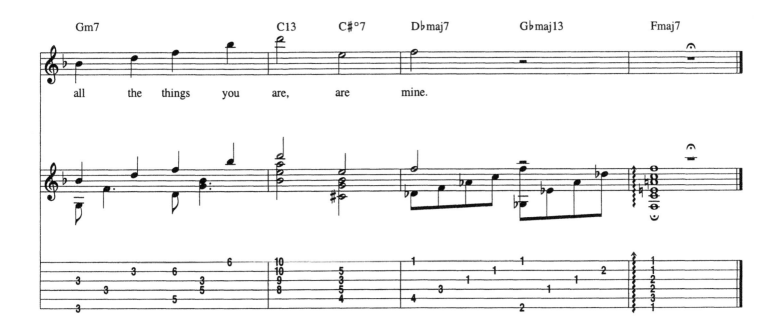

all the things you are, are mine.

The Christmas Song
(Chestnuts Roasting on an Open Fire)

Music and Lyric by Mel Torme and Robert Wells

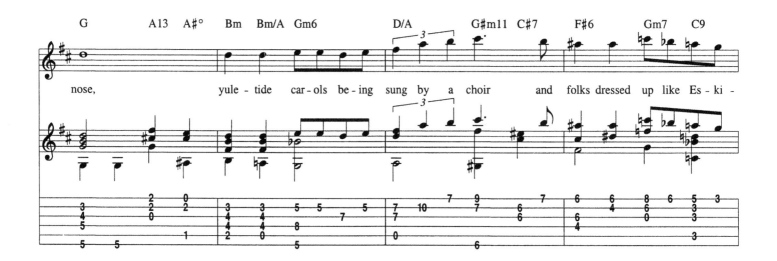

mos.   Ev - 'ry - bod - y knows a tur - key and some mis - tle - toe

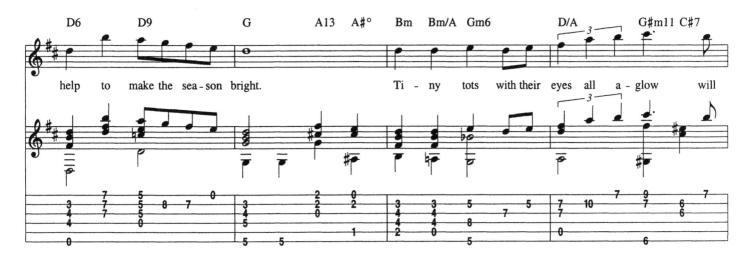

help to make the sea - son bright.   Ti - ny tots with their eyes all a - glow will

find it hard to sleep   to - night.   They know that San - ta's on his

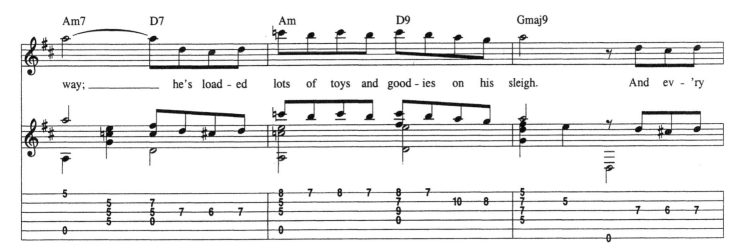

way; _____ he's load - ed lots of toys and good - ies on his sleigh.   And ev - 'ry

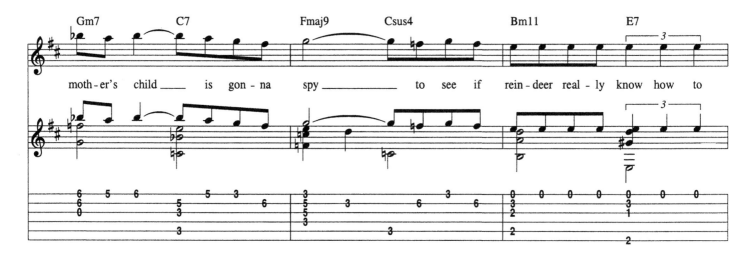

moth-er's child ___ is gon-na spy ___ to see if rein-deer real-ly know how to

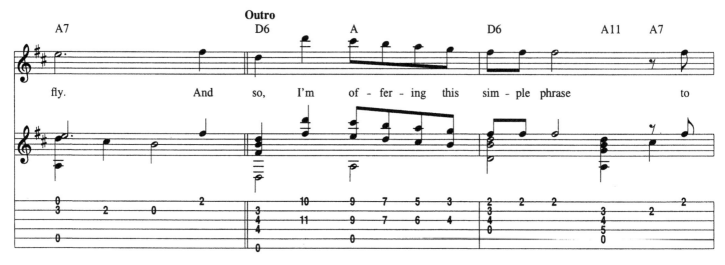

fly.   And so, I'm of-fer-ing this sim-ple phrase   to

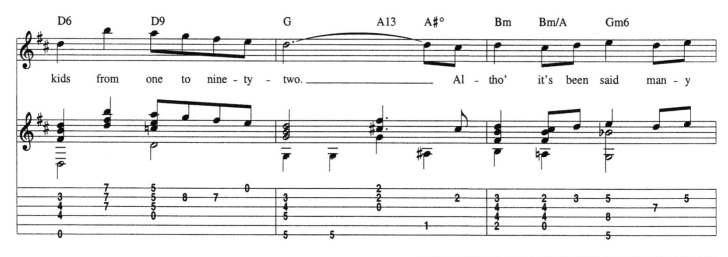

kids from one to nine-ty - two. ___ Al-tho' it's been said man-y

times, man-y ways; "Mer-ry Christ-mas   to you."   you."

Dust in the Wind

Words and Music by Kerry Livgren

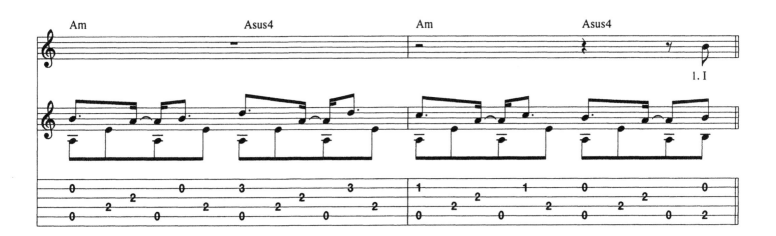

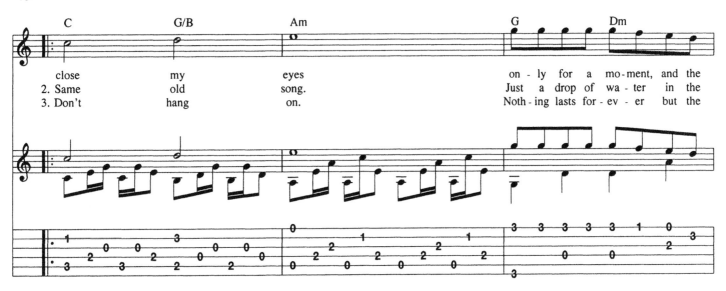

mo - ment's gone. All my dreams
end - less sea. All we do
earth and sky. It slips a - way.

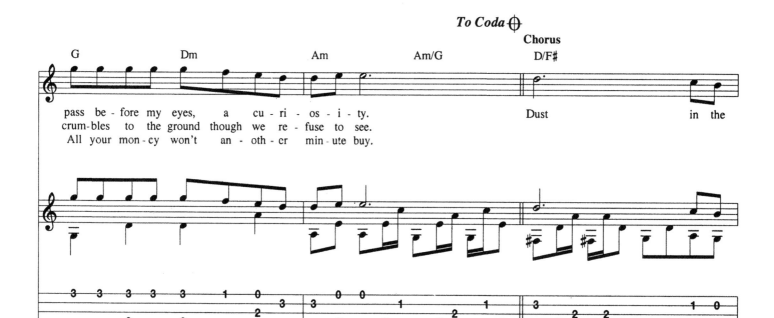

To Coda ⊕

Chorus

pass be - fore my eyes, a cu - ri - os - i - ty. Dust in the
crum - bles to the ground though we re - fuse to see.
All your mon - ey won't an - oth - er min - ute buy.

1.

wind. All they are is dust in the wind.

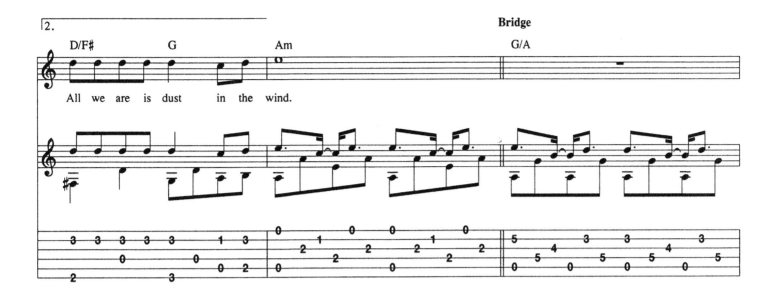

All we are is dust in the wind.

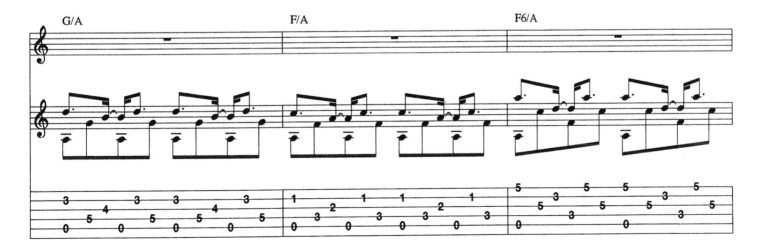

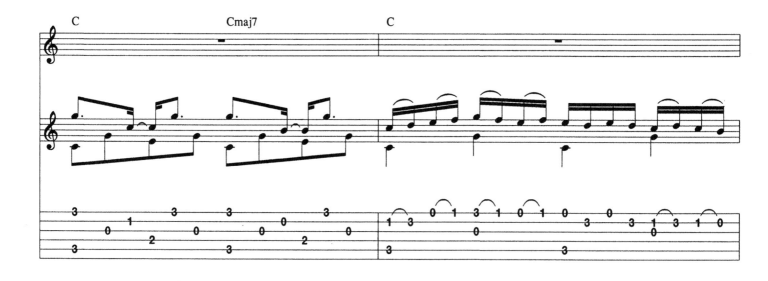

D.S. al Coda

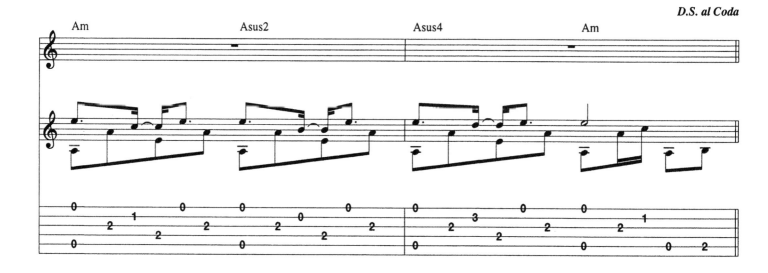

⊕ *Coda*

Chorus

Dust ___ in the wind.

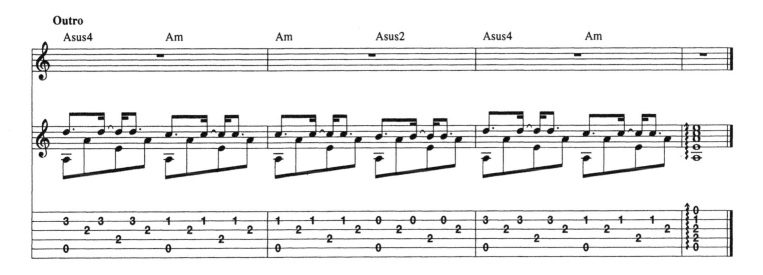

Every Breath You Take

Words and Music by Sting

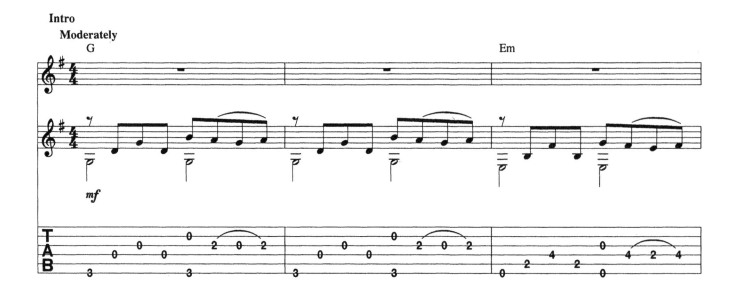

ev-'ry bond _ you break, ___ ev-'ry step _ you take, _ I'll be watch-ing you.

Verse

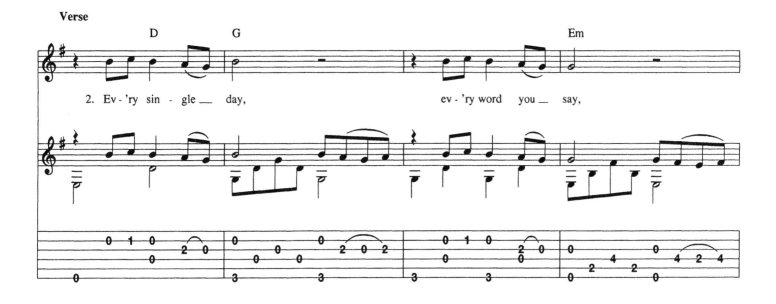

2. Ev - 'ry sin - gle _ day,   ev - 'ry word you _ say,

ev-'ry game _ you play, _ ev-'ry night _ you stay, _ I'll be watch-ing you.

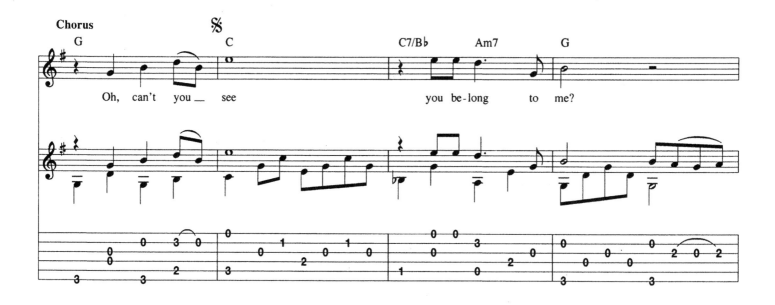

Oh, can't you _ see   you be-long to me?

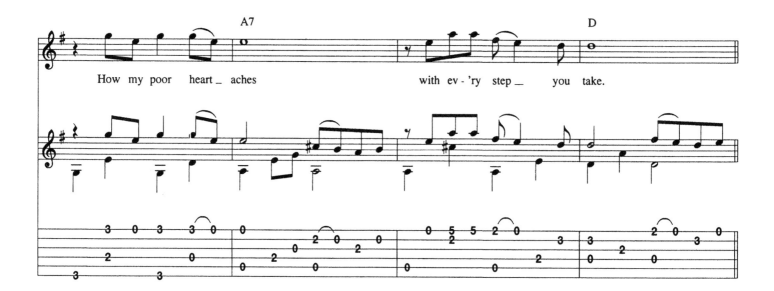

How my poor heart _ aches   with ev-'ry step _ you take.

3. Ev-'ry move you _ make,   ev-'ry vow you _ break,

C   D   Em

ev - 'ry smile you fake, __ ev - 'ry claim you stake, __ I'll be watch - ing you.

Bridge

Eb   F

Since you've gone __ I been lost __ with - out ___ a trace. I dream at night, I can on -

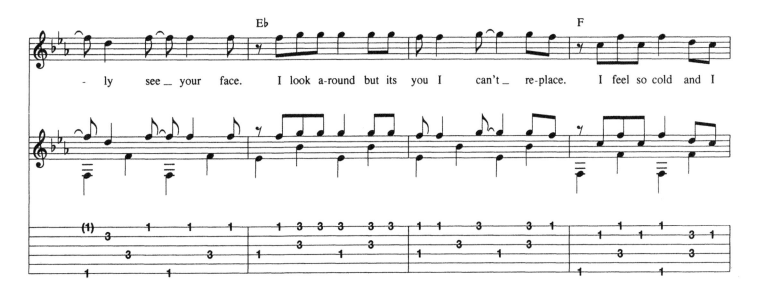

Eb   F

- ly see __ your face. I look a - round but its you I can't __ re - place. I feel so cold and I

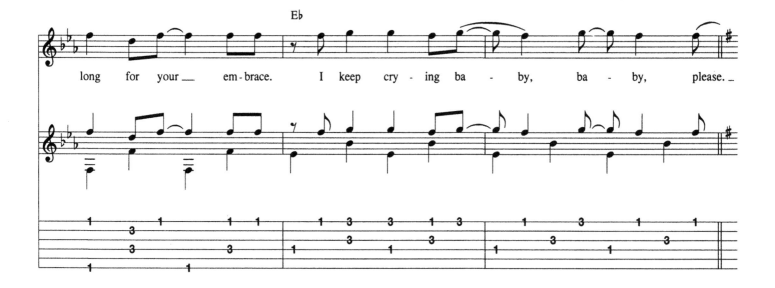

long for your ___ em - brace. I keep cry - ing ba - by, ba - by, please. ___

Interlude

D.S. al Coda

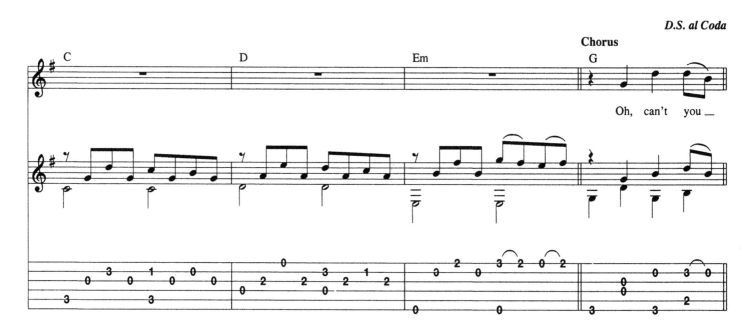

Oh, can't you ___

20

Outro

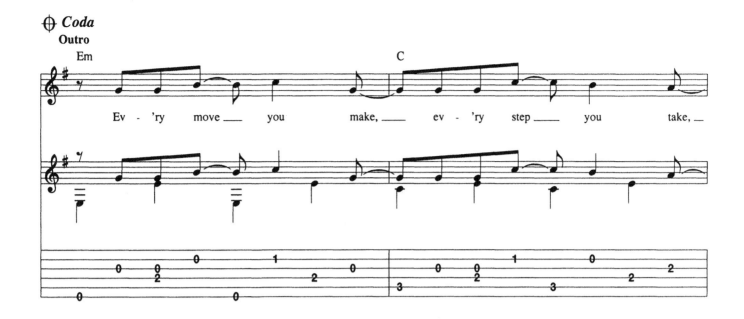

Ev - 'ry move ___ you make, ___ ev - 'ry step ___ you take, ___

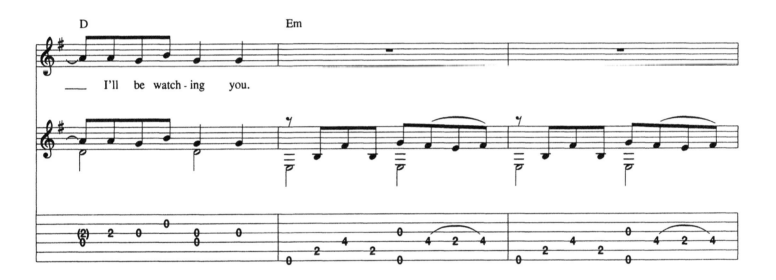

___ I'll be watch - ing you.

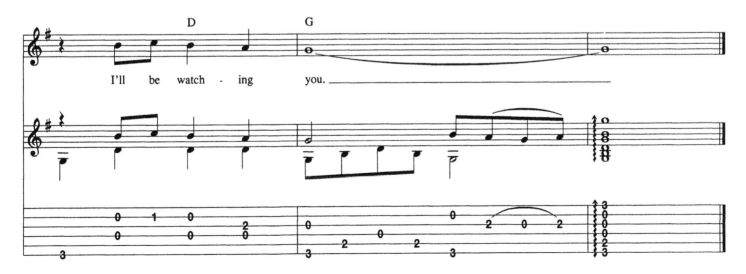

I'll be watch - ing you. ___

Fly Me to the Moon
(In Other Words)

featured in the Motion Picture ONCE AROUND

Words and Music by Bart Howard

Georgia on My Mind

Words by Stuart Gorrell
Music by Hoagy Carmichael

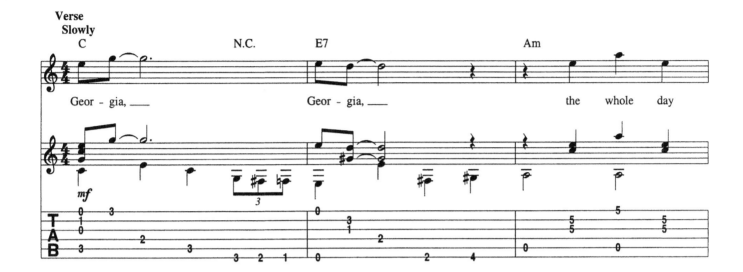

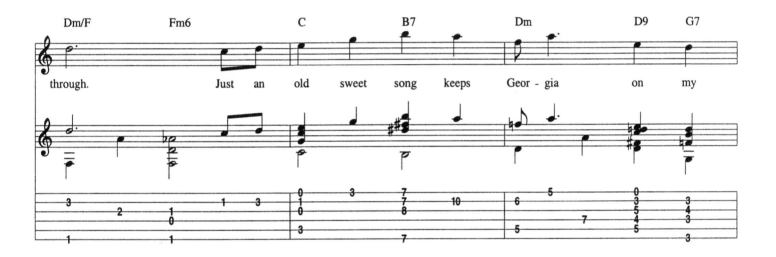

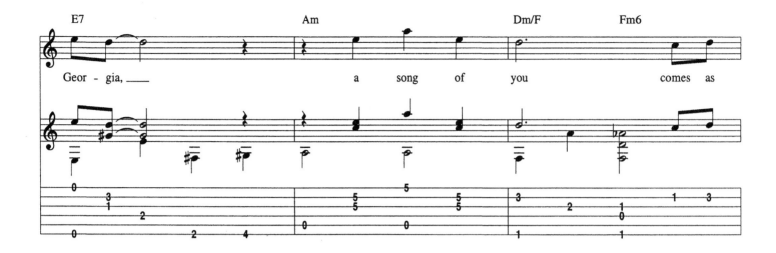

Geor - gia, _____ a song of you comes as

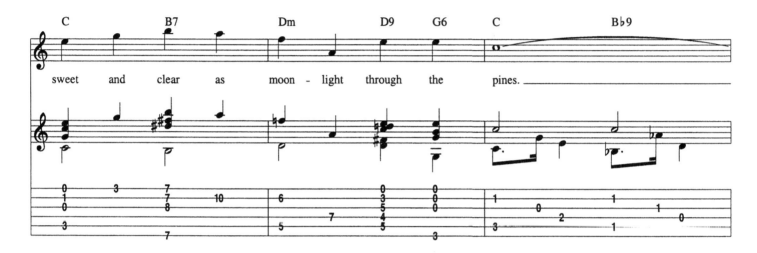

sweet and clear as moon - light through the pines. _____

Bridge

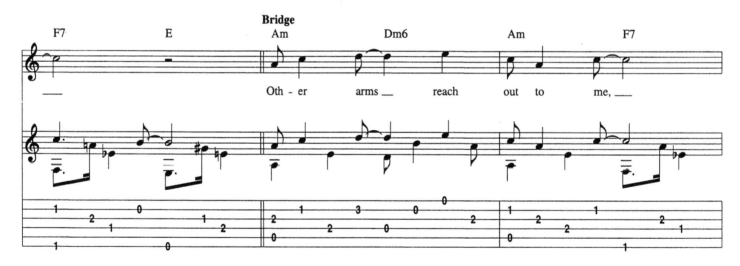

_____ Oth - er arms _____ reach out to me, _____

oth - er eyes _____ smile ten - der - ly. _____ Still in peace - ful

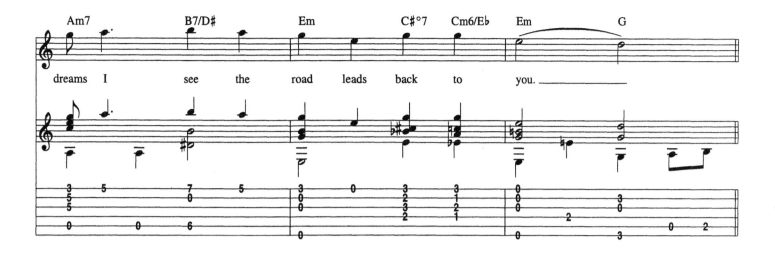

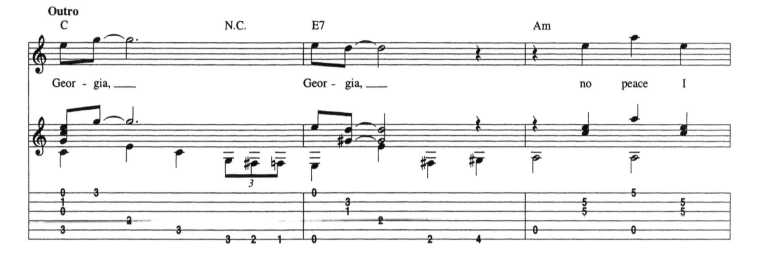

The Girl from Ipanema
(Garôta de Ipanema)

English Words by Norman Gimbel
Original Words by Vinicius de Moraes
Music by Antonio Carlos Jobim

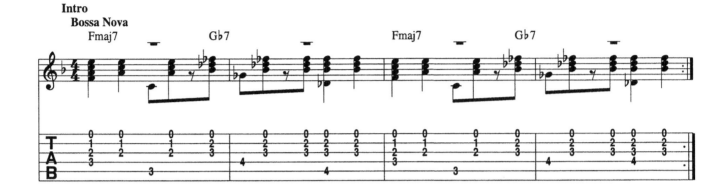

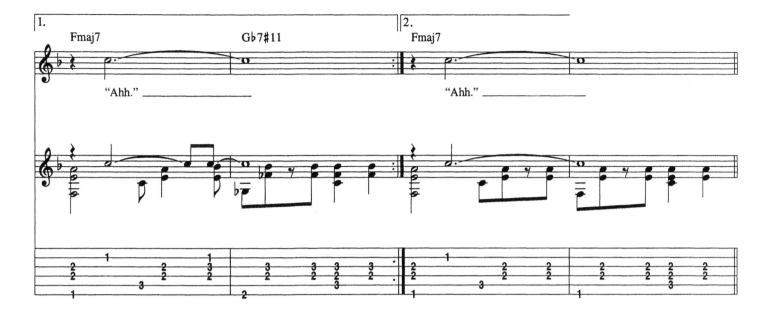

Yes, _____ I would give my heart glad - ly _____ but each day

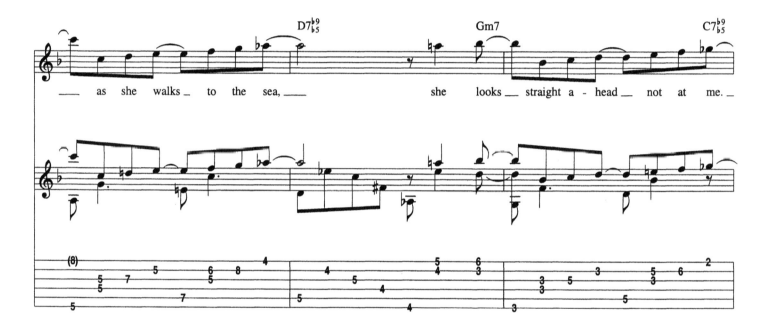

____ as she walks __ to the sea, ____ she looks __ straight a - head __ not at me.

3.Tall and tan and young __ and love - ly the Girl

from Ip - a - ne - ma goes walk-in' and when she pas - ses I smile

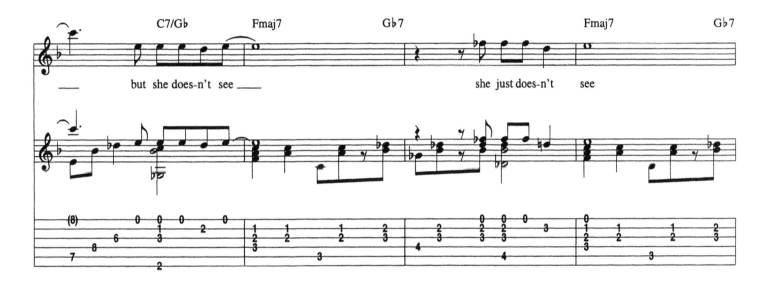

but she does-n't see ___ she just does-n't see

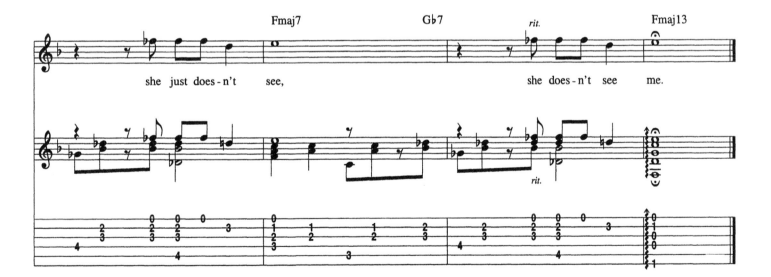

she just does - n't see, she does-n't see me.

Additional Lyrics

2. When she walks it's like a samba
   That swings so smoothe and swags so gentle that
   When she passes, each one she passes goes, "Ahh."

I Just Called to Say I Love You

Words and Music by Stevie Wonder

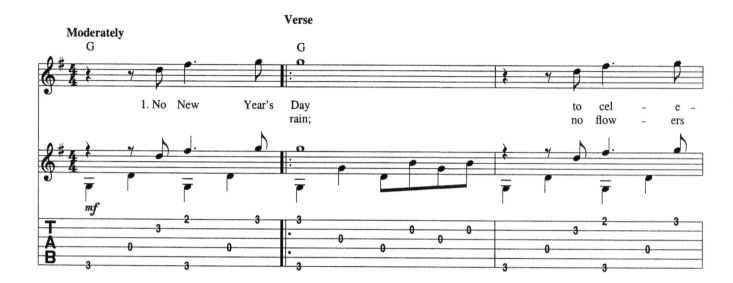

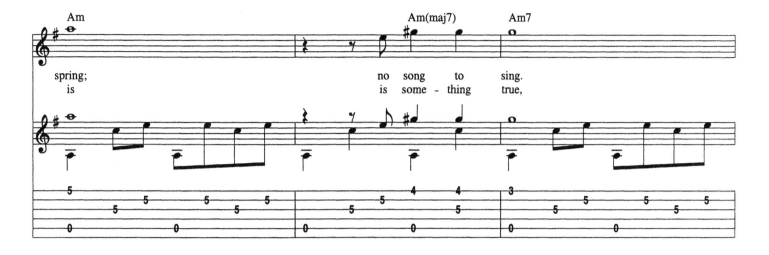

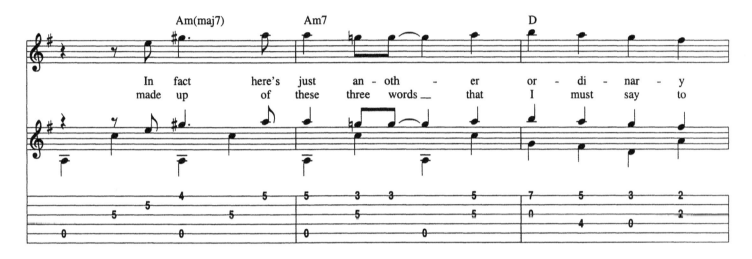

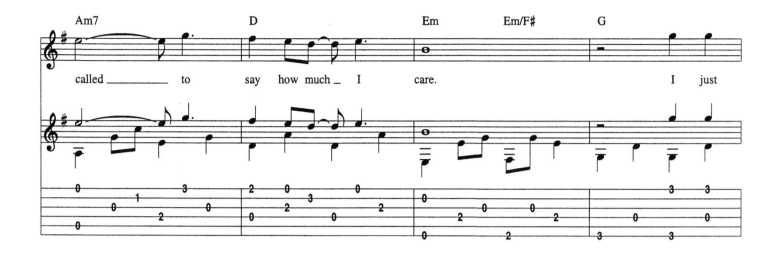

called _____ to say how much _ I care. I just

called _____ to say _____ I love _ you. _ And I

mean it from _ the bot - tom of my heart.

Imagine

Words and Music by John Lennon

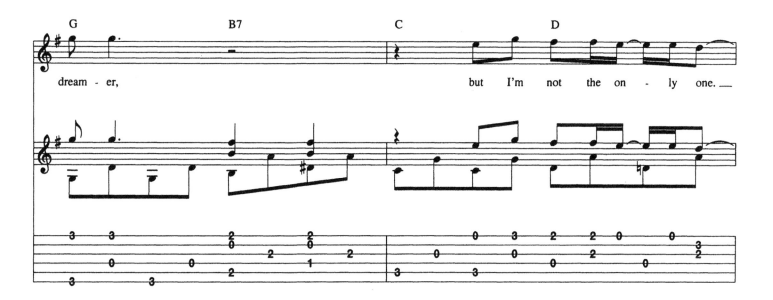

dream - er,   but I'm not the on - ly one. __

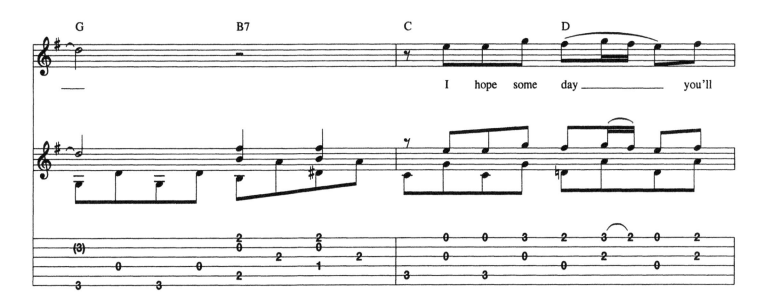

I hope some day _____ you'll

join   us   and the world _____ will   live   as   one.

Just the Way You Are

Words and Music by Billy Joel

Drop "D" Tuning:
①=E ④=D
②=B ⑤=A
③=G ⑥=D

Intro

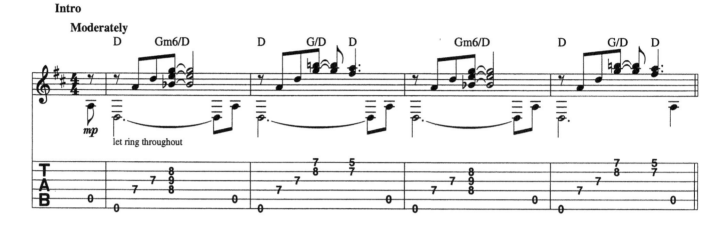

Verse lyrics:
1. Don't go chang-in' to try and please me.
would not leave you in times of trou-ble.
said I love you and that's for-ev-er.
4. See Additonal Lyrics

Lyrics:
You nev-er let me down be-fore.
We nev-er could have come this far.
And this I prom-ise from the heart.

Mmm.

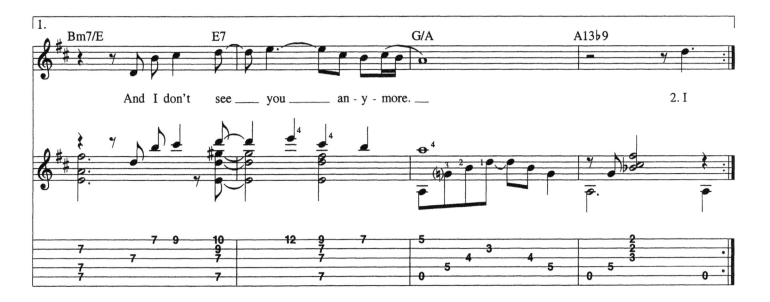

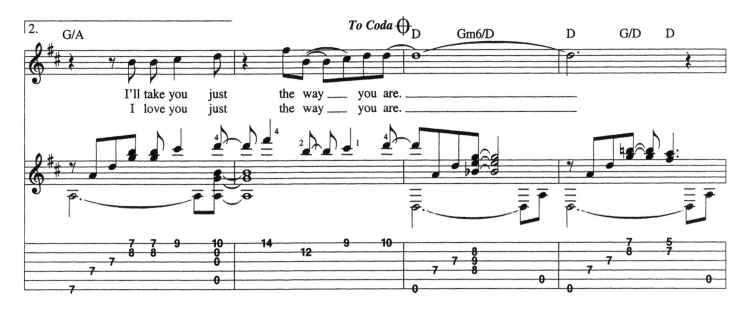

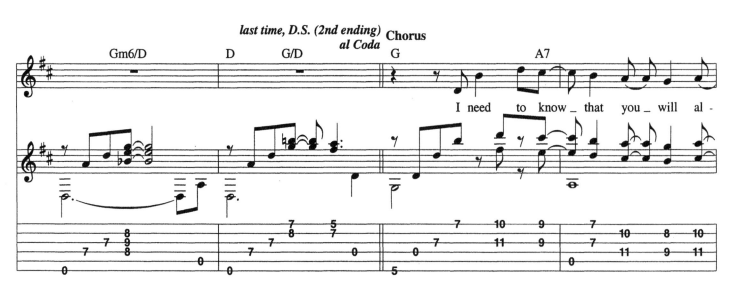

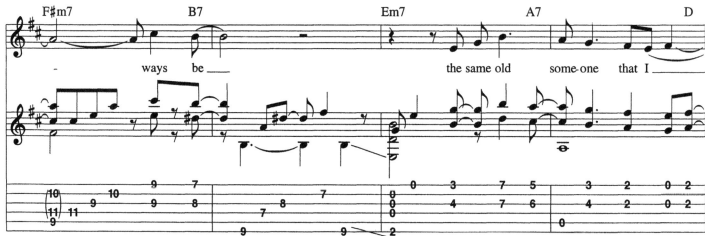

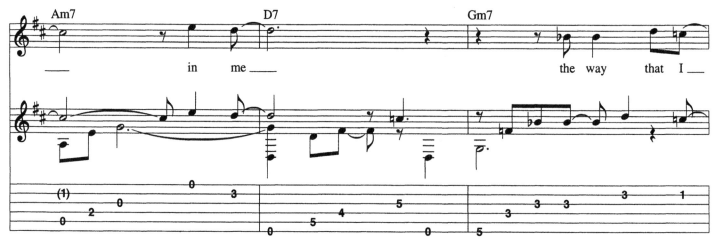

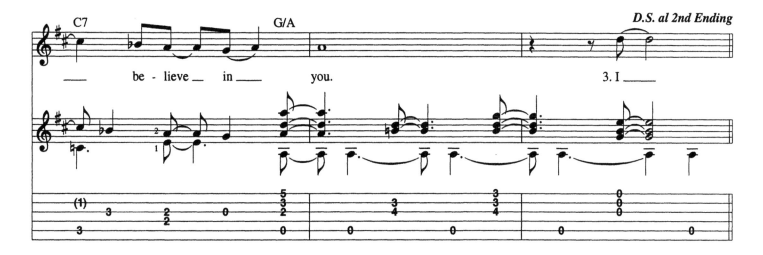

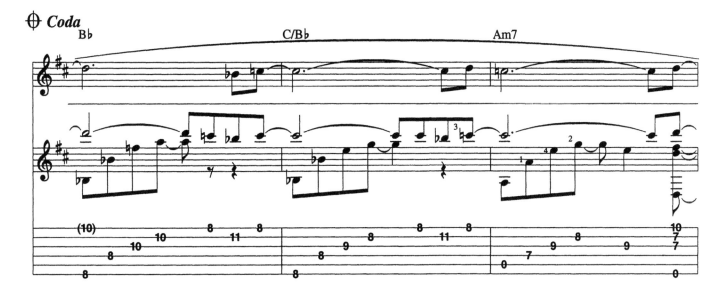

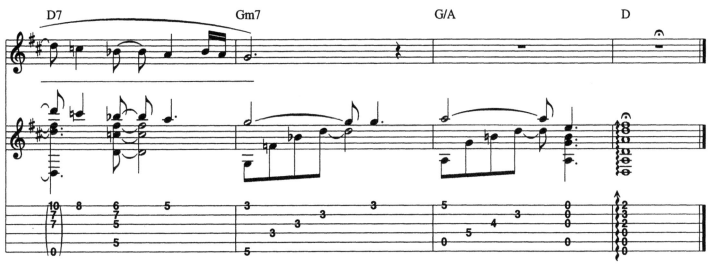

Additonal Lyrics

4 . I don't want clever conversation.
   I never want to work that hard. Mmm...
   I just want someone that I can talk to,
   I want you just the way you are.

Love Me Tender

Words and Music by Elvis Presley and Vera Matson

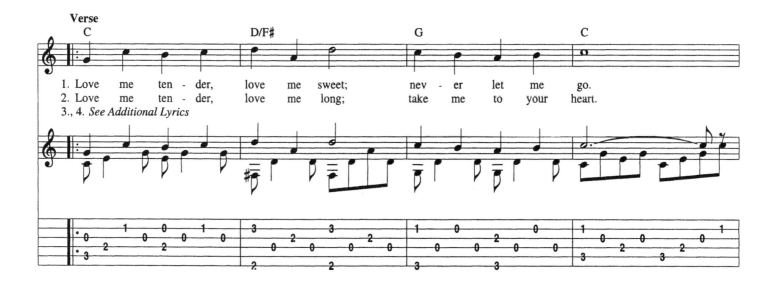

1. Love me ten - der, love me sweet; nev - er let me go.
2. Love me ten - der, love me long; take me to your heart.
3., 4. *See Additional Lyrics*

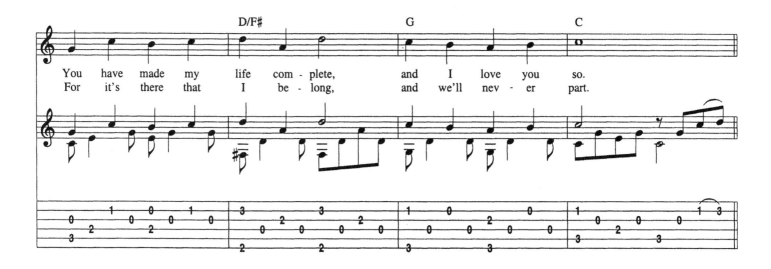

You have made my life com - plete, and I love you so.
For it's there that I be - long, and we'll nev - er part.

Chorus

Love me ten - der, love me true, all my dreams ful - fill.

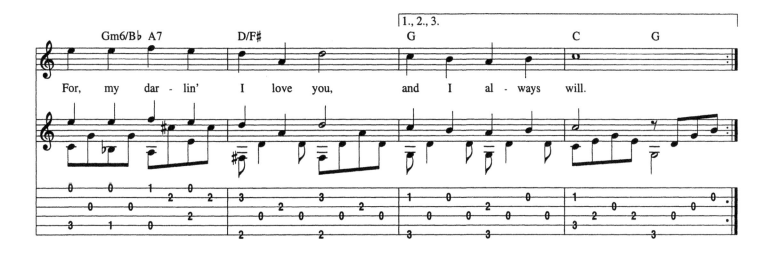

For, my dar - lin' I love you, and I al - ways will.

and I al - ways will.

Additional Lyrics

3. Love me tender, love me dear,
   Tell me you are mine.
   I'll be yours through all the years,
   Till the end of time.

4. When at last my dreams come true,
   Darling this I know:
   Happiness will follow you,
   Ev'rywhere you go.

My Funny Valentine

from BABES IN ARMS

Words by Lorenz Hart
Music by Richard Rodgers

graph - a - ble,   yet you're my fav' - rite work of art.

Bridge

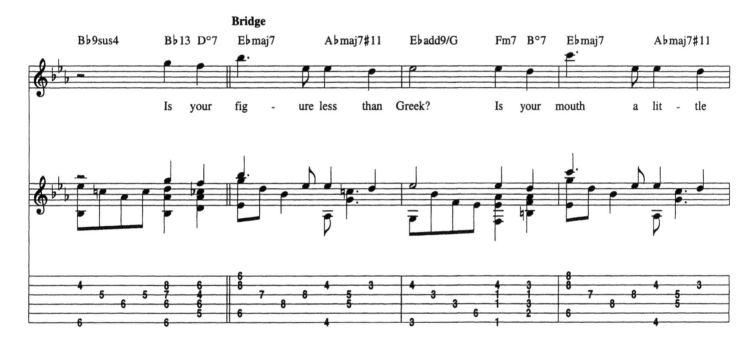

Is   your   fig - ure less   than   Greek?   Is   your   mouth   a   lit - tle

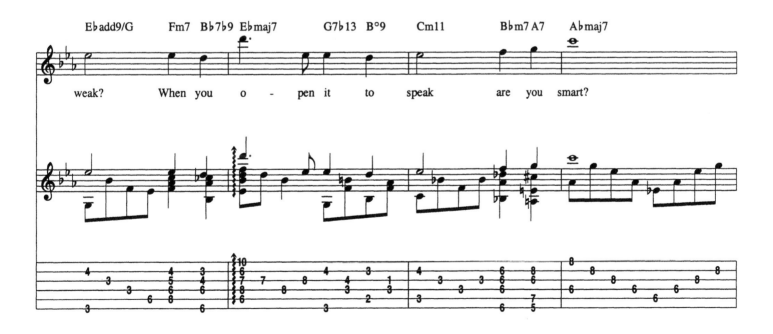

weak?   When   you   o - pen   it   to   speak   are   you   smart?

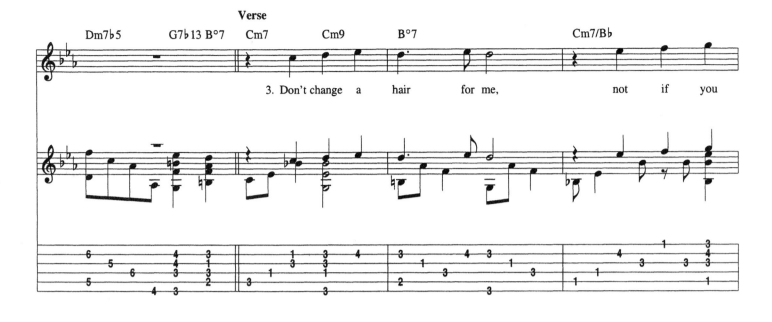

Verse

3. Don't change a hair for me, not if you

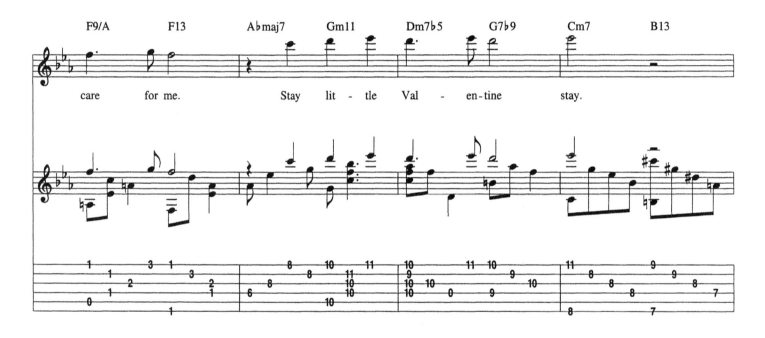

care for me. Stay lit - tle Val - en-tine stay.

Each day is Val - en-tine's Day.

My Heart Will Go On
(Love Theme From 'Titanic')

from the Paramount and Twentieth Century Fox Motion Picture TITANIC

Music by James Horner

Lyric by Will Jennings

Intro
Moderately

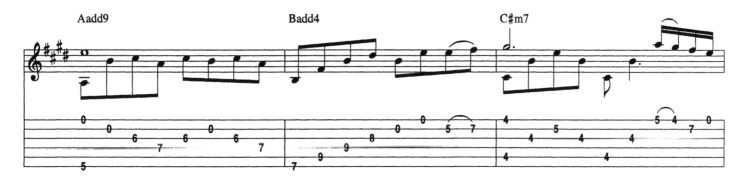

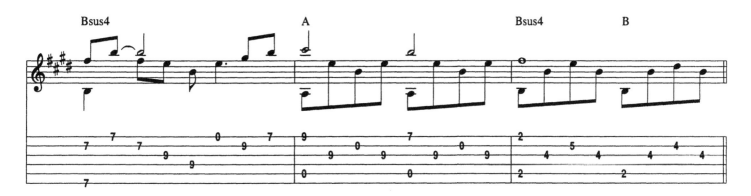

Verse

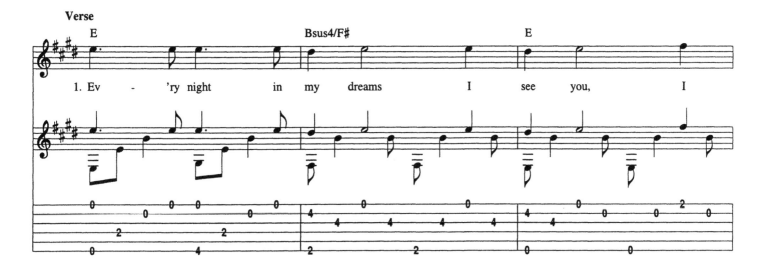

1. Ev - 'ry night in my dreams I see you, I

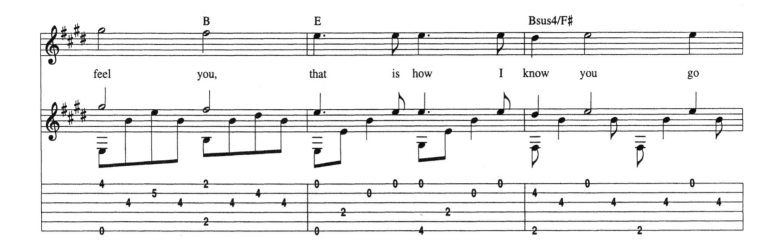

feel you, that is how I know you go

on. Far a - cross the

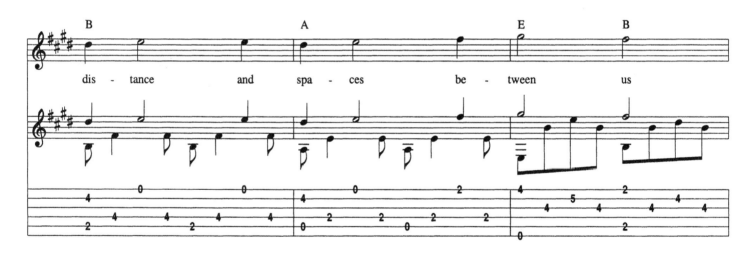

dis - tance and spa - ces be - tween us

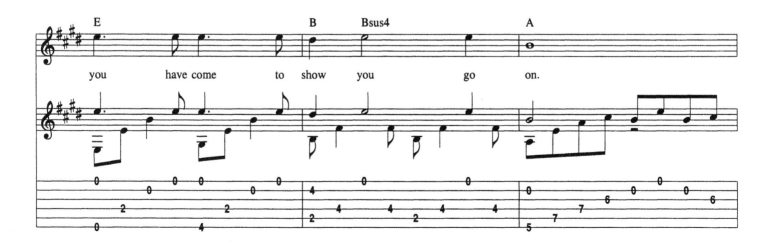

you have come to show you go on.

%. Chorus

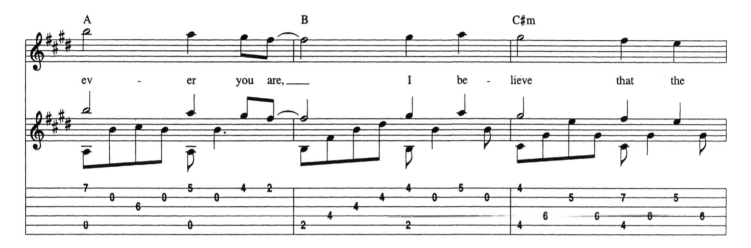

and you're here in my heart, and my heart will go

To Coda ⊕ Interlude

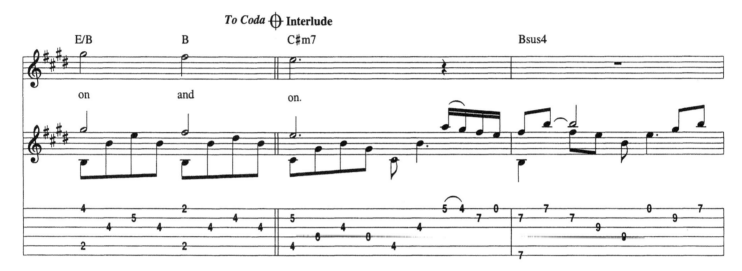

on and on.

Verse

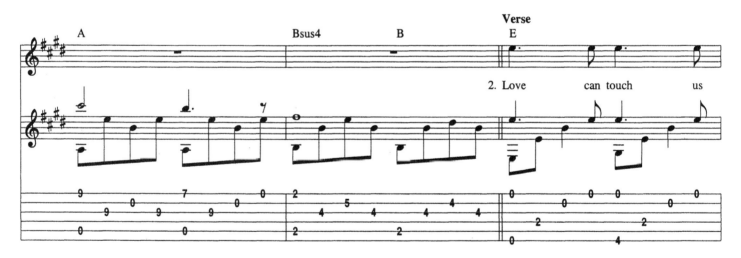

2. Love can touch us

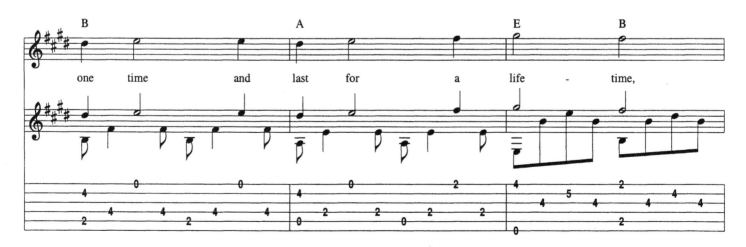

one time and last for a life - time,

and   nev-er   let   go   till   we're   gone.

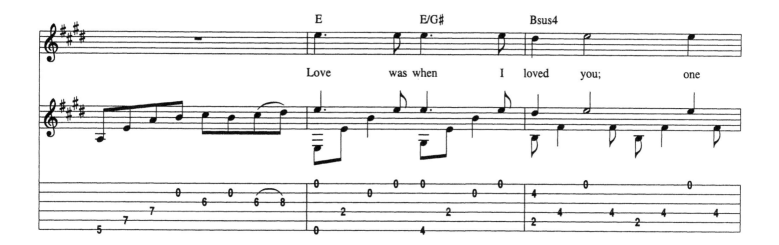

Love   was when   I   loved   you;   one

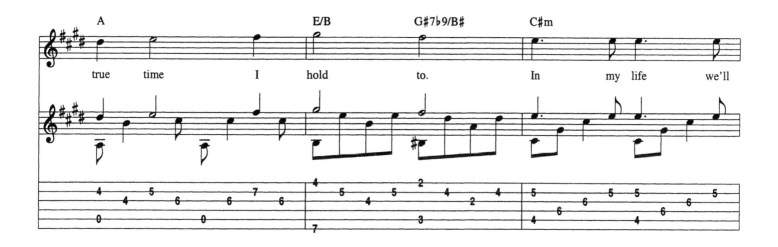

true   time   I   hold   to.   In   my   life   we'll

D.S. al Coda

al - ways   go   on.

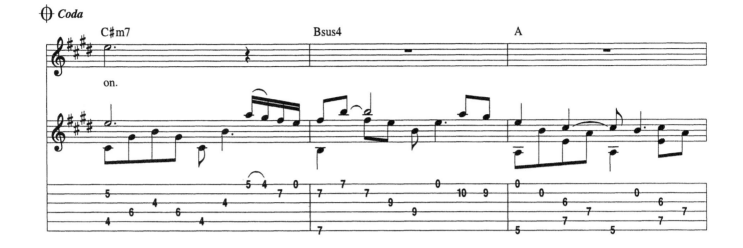

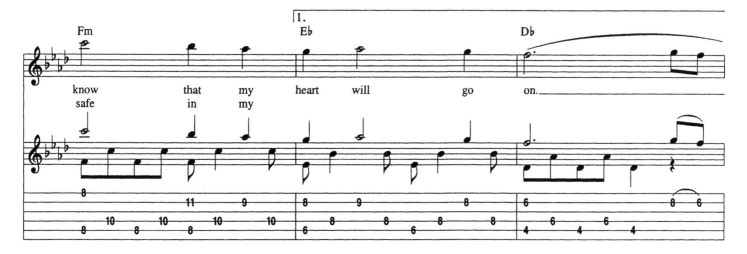

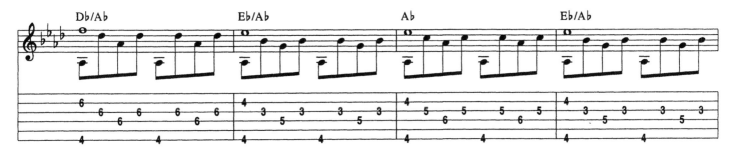

My One and Only Love

Words by Robert Mellin
Music by Guy Wood

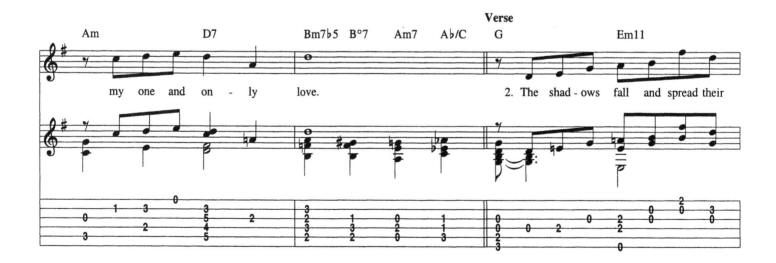

mys - tic charms __ in the hush of night. __ While you're in my arms,

I feel your lips so warm and ten - der, __ my one and on - ly

Bridge

love. The touch __ of your hand __ is like heav - en, __ a

heav - en that I've __ nev - er known. The blush __ of your cheek when -

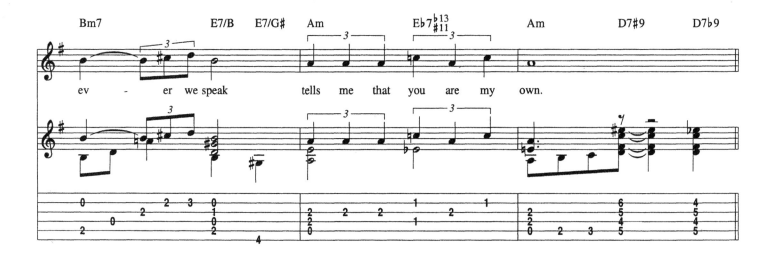

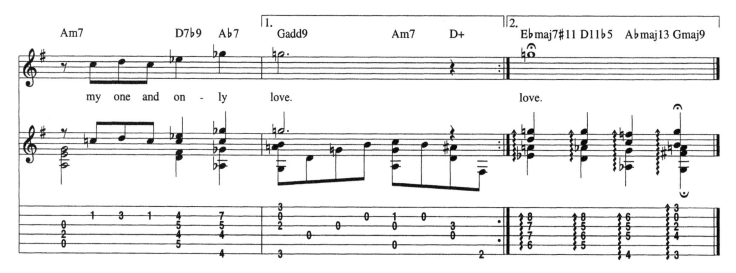

Stella by Starlight

from the Paramount Picture THE UNINVITED

Words by Ned Washington
Music by Victor Young

that rip - ples by a knook where two

lov - ers hide. That great sym - phon - ic

theme; _____ that's Stel - la by Star - light

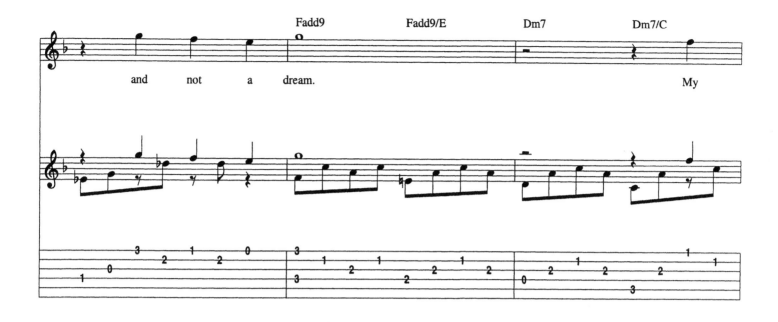

and   not   a   dream.   My

heart   and   I   a - gree   she's   ev - 'ry -

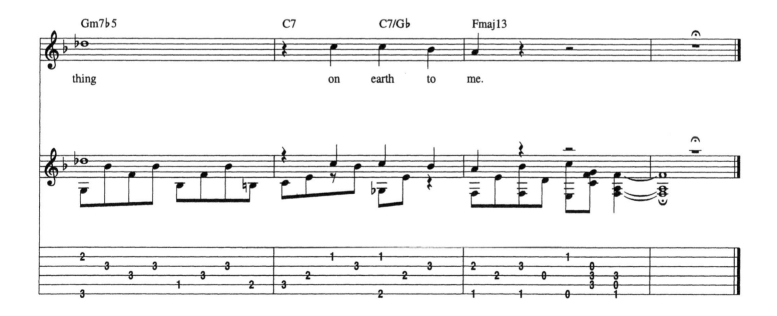

thing   on   earth   to   me.

Tears in Heaven

featured in the Motion Picture RUSH

Words and Music by Eric Clapton and Will Jennings

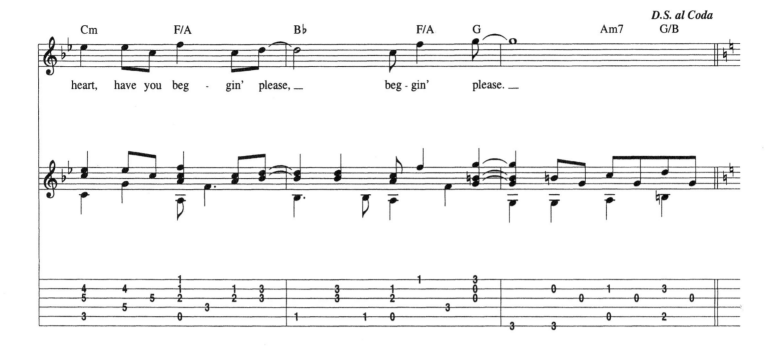

heart, have you beg - gin' please, ___ beg - gin' please. ___

⊕ Coda

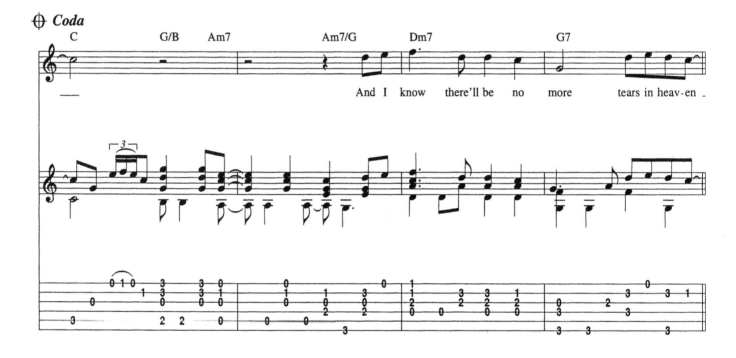

And I know there'll be no more tears in heav-en ___

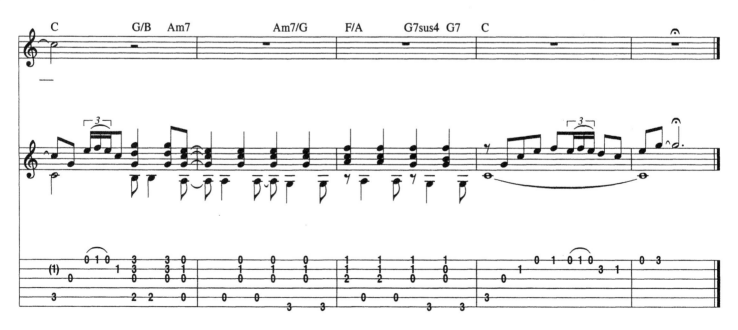

Where Do I Begin
(Love Theme)

from the Paramount Picture LOVE STORY

Words by Carl Sigman
Music by Francis Lai

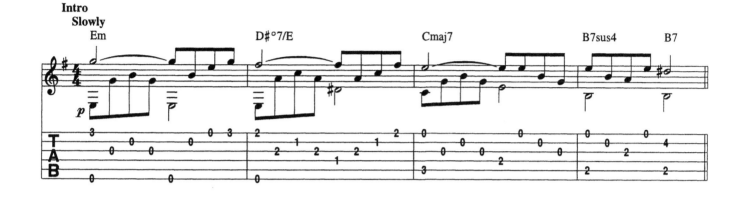

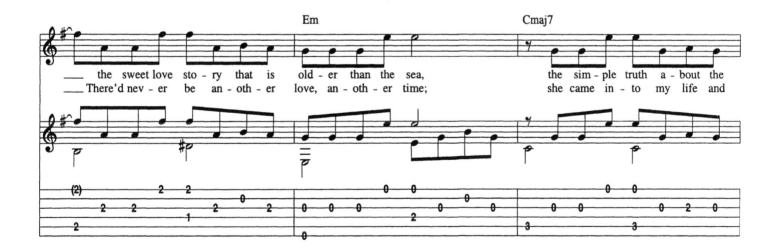

love she brings to me? _____ Where do I start?
made the liv - ing fine. _____

She fills my heart. _____ She fills my heart _____ with ver - y

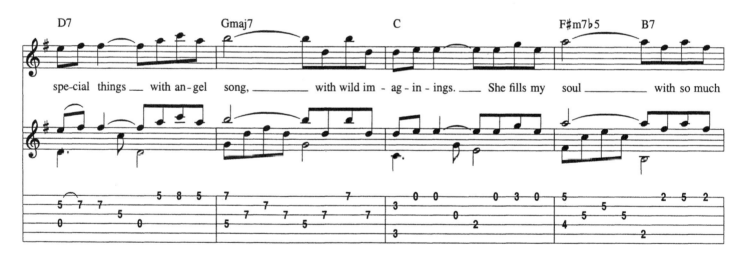

spe - cial things _____ with an - gel song, _____ with wild im - ag - in - ings. _____ She fills my soul _____ with so much

love that an - y - where I go _____ I'm nev - er lone - ly, _____ with her a - long, _____ who could be

64

lone - ly?___ I reach for her hand, ___ it's al-ways there. ___

Outro

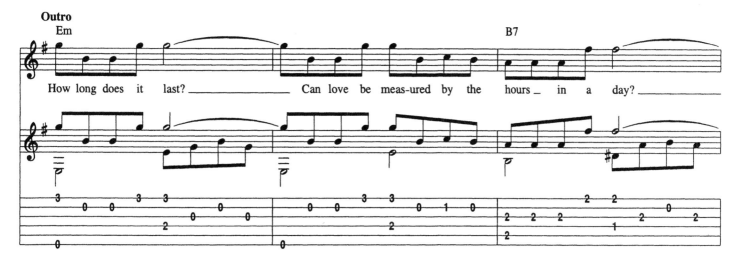

How long does it last? ___ Can love be meas-ured by the hours _ in a day? ___

___ I have no an-swers now, but this much I can say: I know I'll need her till the

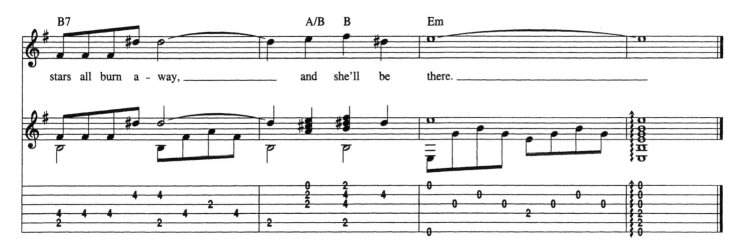

stars all burn a - way, ___ and she'll be there. ___

Unchained Melody

featured in the Motion Picture GHOST

Lyric by Hy Zaret
Music by Alex North

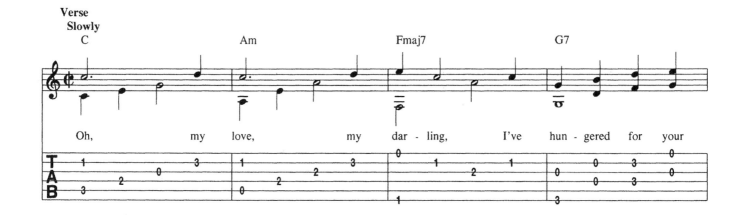

Oh, my love, my dar-ling, I've hun-gered for your

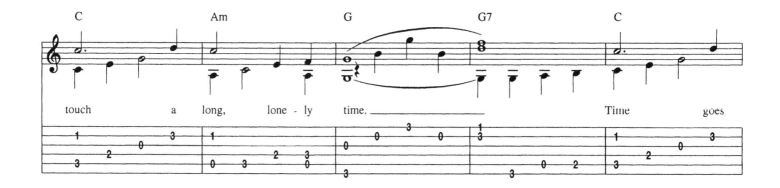

touch a long, lone-ly time. _____ Time goes

by so slow-ly and time can do so much. Are you still

mine? _____ I need your love. _____ I need your love. _____

Fine

Cmaj7   Dm   Dm7   G   C

God - speed your love _____ to me. _____

F   G   F   E♭

Lone - ly riv - ers flow _____ to the sea, _____ to the sea,
Lone - ly moun - tains gaze _____ at the stars, _____ at the stars,

F   G   C

to the o - pen arms _____ of the sea. _____
wait - ing for the dawn _____ of the day. _____

F   G   F   E♭

Lone - ly riv - ers sigh, _____ "Wait for me, _____ to the me!
All a - lone I gaze _____ at the stars, _____ at the stars,

1.   2.

D.C. al Fine

F   G   C

I'll be com - ing home, ___ wait for me!" _____
dream - ing of my love _____ far a - way. _____

Yesterday

Words and Music by John Lennon and Paul McCartney

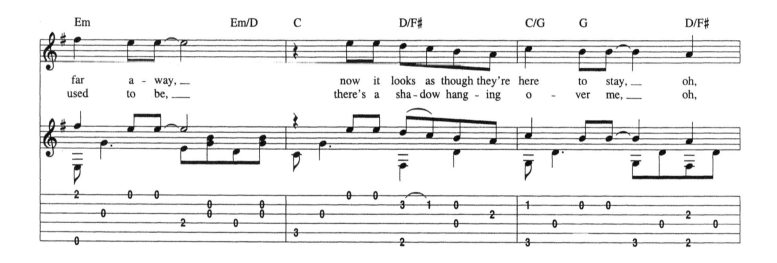

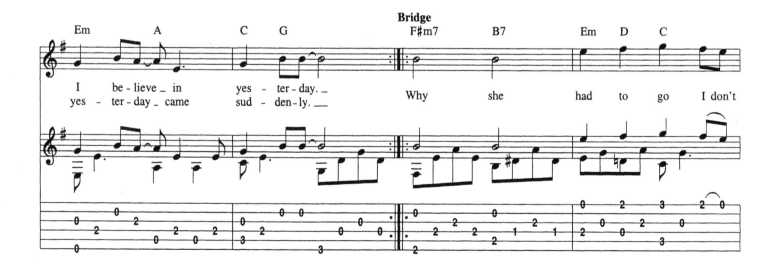

You Needed Me

Words and Music by Randy Goodrum

Chorus

dig - ni - ty. Some - how you need - ed me.
truth a - gain. You e - ven called me friend.

You gave me strength to stand a -

lone a - gain to face the world out on my own a - gain. You put me

high up - on a ped - es - stal so high that I can al - most see e -

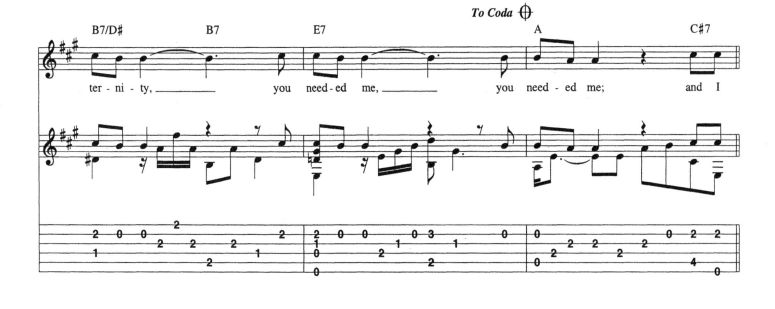

fin - 'lly found some - one who real - ly cares.

2. You held my

⊕ *Coda*

need - ed me.

You need - ed me,

you

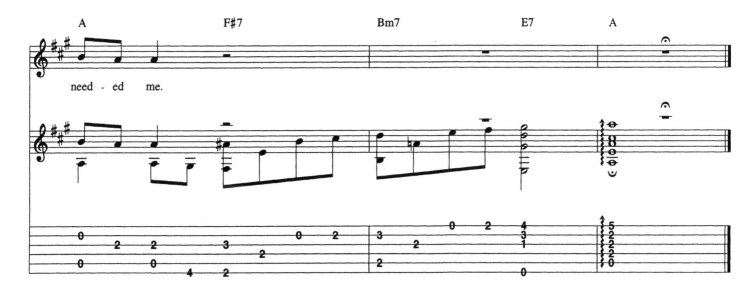

need - ed me.

Your Song

Words and Music by Elton John and Bernie Taupin

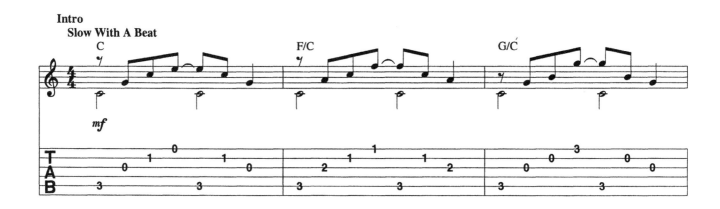

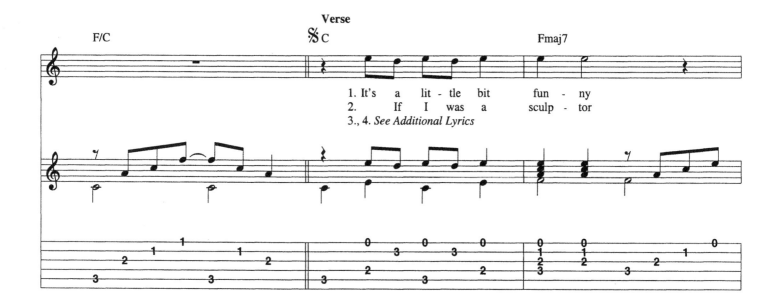

eas - i - ly hide, _____ I don't have much
trav - el - in' show. _____ I know ___ it's not

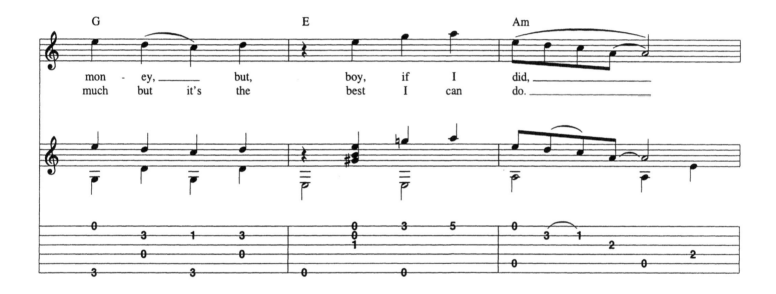

mon - ey, ___ but, boy, if I did, _____
much but it's the best I can do. _____

I'd buy a big house where _____ we both could
My gift is my house song and _____

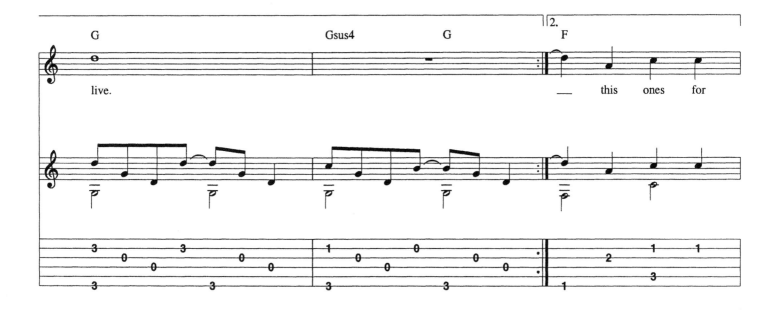

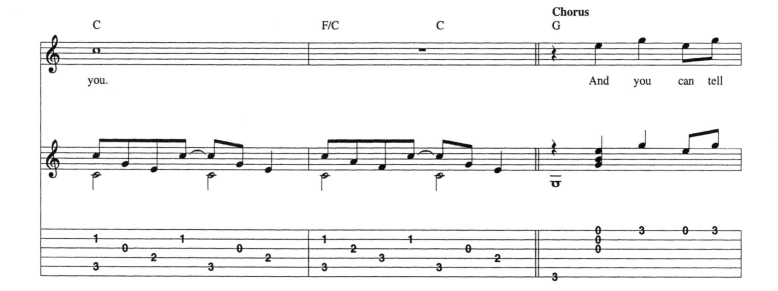

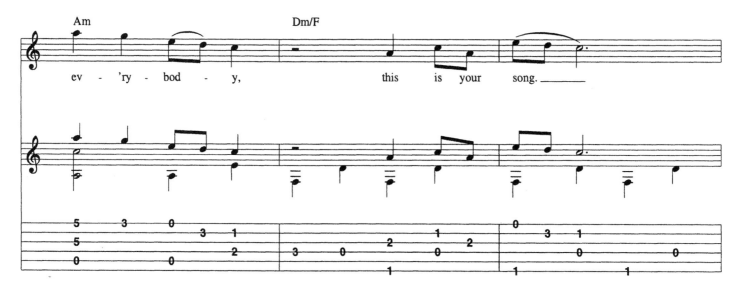

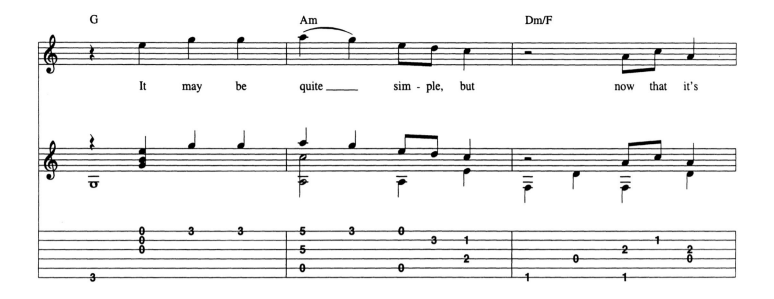

It may be quite _____ sim - ple, but now that it's

To Coda ⊕

done, _____ I hope you don't mind, I hope you don't mind _____

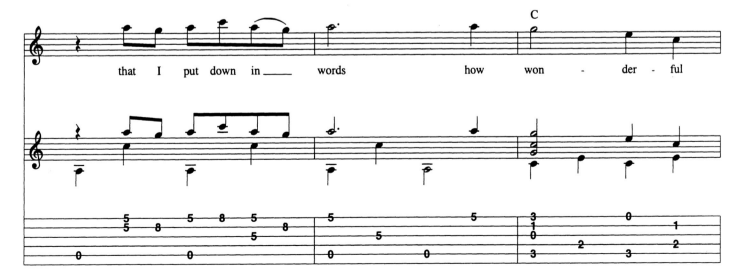

that I put down in _____ words how won - der - ful

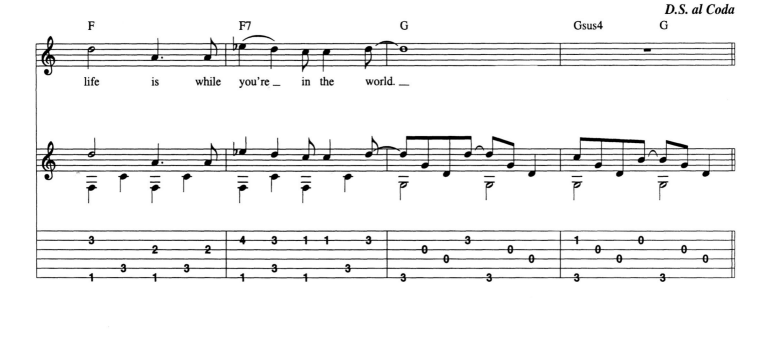

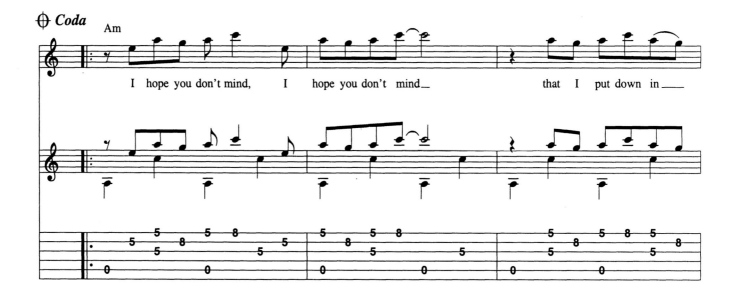

you're ___ in the world. ___

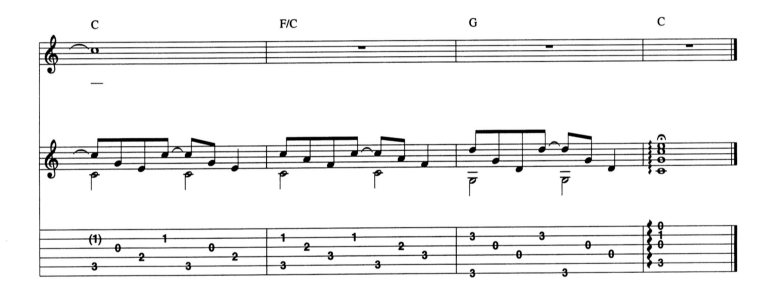

Additional Lyrics

3. I sat on the roof and kicked off the moss.
   Well a few of the verses, well they've got me quite cross,
   But the sun been quite kind while I wrote this song.
   It's for people like you that keep it turned on.

4. So excuse me for forgetting, but these things I do.
   You see, I've forgotten if they're green or they're blue.
   Anyway, the thing is what I really mean,
   Yours are the sweetest eyes I've ever seen.